**Once Loyal Friends...
Now Mortal Enemies**

**A wild frenzy suddenly overtakes the
dispassionate Spock, crushing his
Vulcan self control and pushing him
to the brink of madness.**

**And Kirk is forced to face his closest
friend in mortal combat. A savage
battle from which only one can
emerge alive to tell the fantastic
story of...**

AMOK TIME

OTHER **STAR TREK FOTONOVELS**[TM]
YOU WILL ENJOY—

STAR TREK™*

AMOK TIME

written by **THEODORE STURGEON**

adapted from the television series
created by **GENE RODDENBERRY**

BANTAM BOOKS · TORONTO · NEW YORK · LONDON ·

RLI: $\dfrac{\text{VLM 6 (VLR 5–7)}}{\text{IL 5+}}$

AMOK TIME
A Bantam Book / October 1978

Art Direction
Michael Parish, Los Angeles

Star Trek™ *designates a trademark of*
Paramount Pictures Corporation.

Fotonovel™ *designates a trademark of*
Mandala Productions.

ISBN 0-553-12012-3

Published simultaneously in the United States and Canada

Bantam Books are published by Bantam Books, Inc. Its trademark, consisting of the words "Bantam Books" and the por-
trayal of a bantam, is registered in the United States Patent
Office and in other countries. Marca Registrada. Bantam
Books, Inc., 666 Fifth Avenue, New York, New York 10019.

PRINTED IN THE UNITED STATES OF AMERICA
0 9 8 7 6 5 4 3 2 1

Dear Mandala Staff,

I recently had the opportunity to see one of your "Star Trek" Fotonovels and I wanted to drop you a note to tell you how much I enjoyed it.

The format that you have pioneered in the United States is remarkable. Looking over the pictures and reading the dialogue made me feel as if I were once again on the Starship. Why, I could almost hear Kirk calling me down in Sickbay.

I don't believe anyone of us in the cast had the slightest notion of the enormous impact our show would make on television viewers all over the world and your books insure that the whole phenomena is still going strong.

It has been an extraordinary experience being a part of a show that has touched the lives of so many people in so many ways and therefore, it is personally gratifying that you have chosen "Star Trek" to launch your new series of Fotonovels. Best of luck in the future.

Sincerely,

DeForest Kelley

CAST LIST

James T. Kirk, Captain
William Shatner

A man whose independent nature and compassionate heart make him a natural leader. His overriding concern is always the well-being of his ship and its crew.

Spock, First Officer
Leonard Nimoy

Chief Science Officer. Of Vulcan and Terran heritage, which accounts for his analytical mind and extraordinary strength. Logic and reason rule his life.

Leonard McCoy, M.D., Lt. Commander
DeForest Kelley

Senior Ship's Surgeon, head of Life Sciences Department. Though surrounded by the most advanced equipment the Federation can offer, he still practices medicine more with his heart than his head.

Sulu
Chief
Helmsman
George Takei

**Uhura,
Lt. Communi-
cations Officer**
Nichelle
Nichols

**Pavel
Chekov,
Ensign
Navigator**
Walter Koenig

**Christine
Chapel**
Head Nurse
Majel Barrett

T'Pring
Arlene Martel

T'Pau
Celia Lovsky

Stonn
Lawrence
Montaigne

Vulcans

Charles Palmer
Joe Paz
Russ Peek
Mark Russell
Mauri Russell
Frank Vinci
Gary Wright

AMOK TIME

SPACE:
THE FINAL FRONTIER

THESE ARE THE VOYAGES OF THE STARSHIP "ENTERPRISE." ITS FIVE YEAR MISSION: TO EXPLORE STRANGE NEW WORLDS...TO SEEK OUT NEW LIFE AND NEW CIVILIZATIONS...TO BOLDLY GO WHERE NO MAN HAS GONE BEFORE.

CAPTAIN'S LOG:
STARDATE 3372.7

EN ROUTE TO ALTAIR VI, THE "ENTERPRISE" IS ONE OF THREE FEDERATION STARSHIPS SCHEDULED TO ATTEND THE INAUGURATION CEREMONIES OF THE NEW PRESIDENT OF THE ALTAIR SYSTEM. OUR MISSION: A DIPLOMATIC SHOW OF FEDERATION FORCE AND FRIENDSHIP.

Captain, got a minute?

That's about **all** I've got, Doctor. What can I do for you?

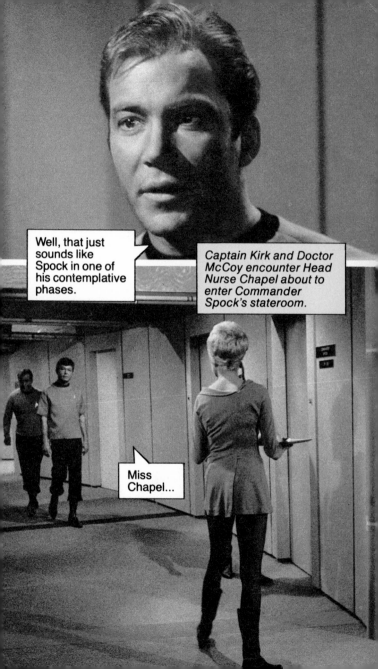

Spock said **that?**

Hearing a shout from within Spock's quarters, Kirk and McCoy turn to see Nurse Chapel dash into the corridor, just ahead of the plomeek soup, thrown after her.

Sensitive to the pain underlying Spock's aberrant behavior, Kirk is determined to know the nature of his friend's distress.

Shortly, in the privacy of Spock's quarters...

All right Spock! Let's have it.

It is undignified for a woman to play servant to a man that is not hers. I did not wish—

I'm more interested in your request for shore leave. In all the years that I've known you, you've never asked for leave of any sort. In fact, you've refused them. Why now?

I suppose most of us overlook the fact that even Vulcans aren't indestructible.

CAPTAIN'S LOG:

STARDATE 3372.8

ON COURSE, ON SCHEDULE, BOUND FOR ALTAIR VI VIA VULCAN. FIRST OFFICER SPOCK SEEMS TO BE UNDER STRESS. HE HAS REQUESTED AND BEEN GRANTED SHORE LEAVE. SHIP'S SURGEON MCCOY HAS HIM UNDER MEDICAL SURVEILLANCE.

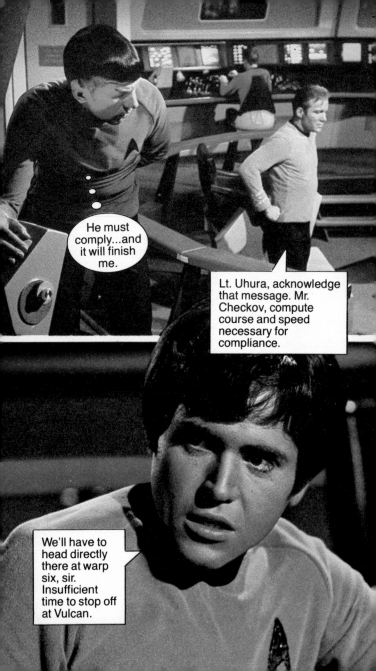

CAPTAIN'S LOG:

SUPPLEMENTAL ENTRY

IN ACCORDANCE WITH A SIGNAL FROM ADMIRAL KOMACK, WE HAVE ALTERED OUR COURSE TO HEAD DIRECTLY FOR ALTAIR VI, PRECLUDING OUR STOP-OVER ON VULCAN.

Alone in his quarters, Kirk weighs alternatives...

I can't just let Spock down... there must be some way to get him to Vulcan...

In the privacy of the turbo elevator...
You changed course for Vulcan, Mr. Spock. Why?
Changed the course?
Could I have done that?
Do you deny it?

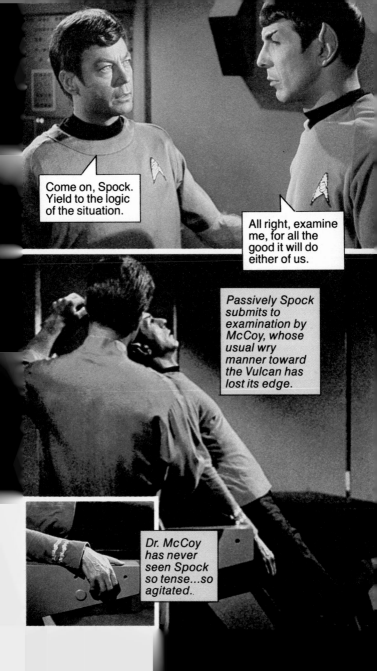

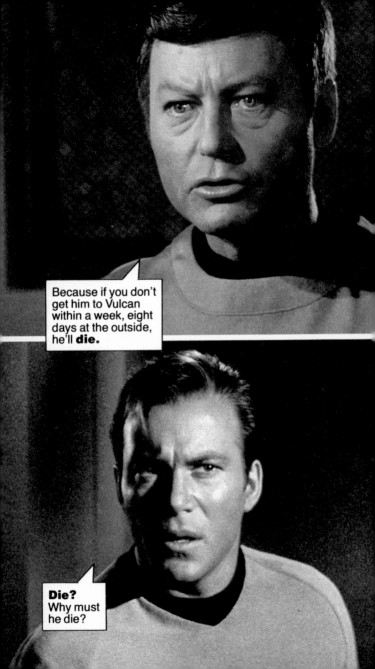

There's a growing imbalance of body functions and I can't trace it down in my bio-comps. For some reason Spock won't tell me what it is. But if it isn't stopped, the physical and emotional pressures will simply kill him.

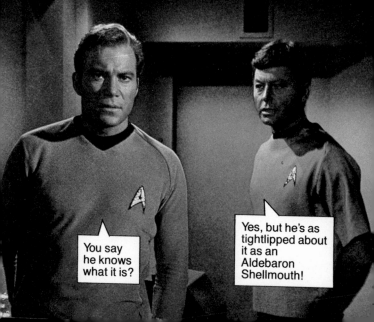

You say he knows what it is?

Yes, but he's as tightlipped about it as an Aldebaron Shellmouth!

In his stateroom, First Officer Spock sits wrapped in thought, studying a screen...

...absorbed in an image somehow linked with the agony welling within him.

At the sound of his door buzzer, Spock shuts off the screen and admits Captain Kirk, whose voice betrays his concern.

Mr. Spock, McCoy has given me his medical evaluation of your condition.

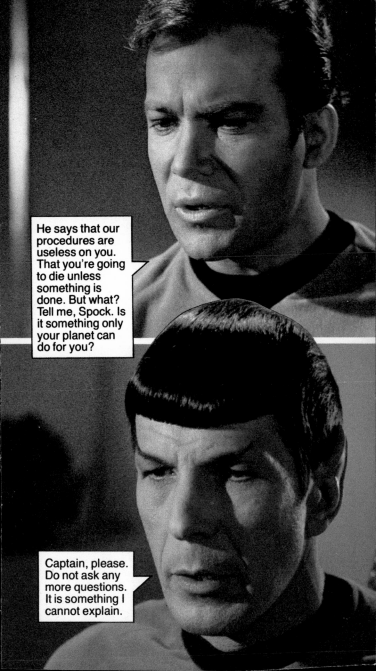

Haven't you ever wondered how Vulcans choose their mates? You've probably assumed it is done quite logically. It is not. We shield it with ritual and custom shrouded in antiquity. You humans have no conception. It brings a madness which rips away any veneer of civilization. It is the pon farr—the time of mating.

From McCoy's office, Kirk speaks to Komack.

Admiral Komack, I'm aware that I'm making a most unusual request, but you must give me permission to divert to Vulcan.

That, I cannot do. Altair is just putting itself together after a long interplanetary conflict. Our appearance there is a demonstration of friendship and strength which will cause ripples clear to the Klingon Empire.

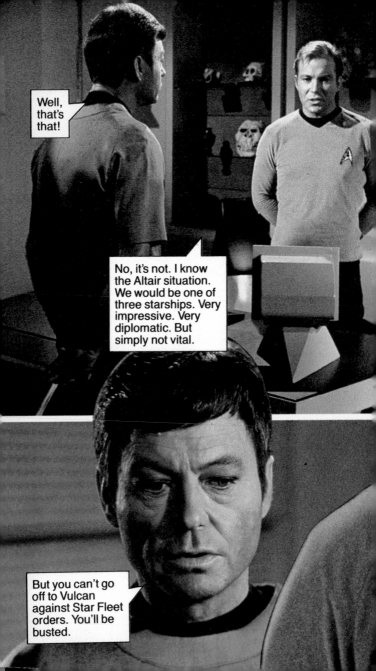

Once Kirk makes a decision, action follows thought without hesitation.

Bridge, Navigation. Mr. Chekov, lay in a course for Vulcan. Tell Engineering I want warp eight or better. Push her for all she'll take.

Though possessed of physical strength beyond that of humans, Spock's hand is gentle as he takes her tear on his finger.

With Spock's life at stake, the Enterprise *is bound for Vulcan in direct contravention of Star Fleet orders. Captain Kirk is aware that this may be his last command.*

Nearing Vulcan, the Enterprise *approaches orbit, and Kirk, Spock and McCoy have a moment alone as they take the turbo-lift to the bridge.*

It's obvious that you've surmised my problem, Doctor. My compliments on your insight.

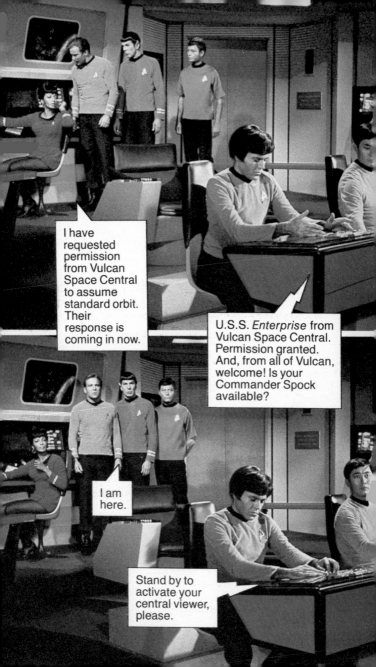

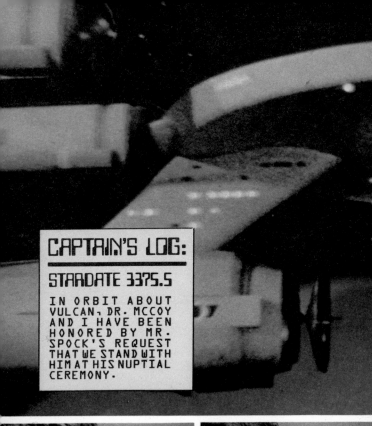

CAPTAIN'S LOG:

STARDATE 3375.5

IN ORBIT ABOUT VULCAN, DR. MCCOY AND I HAVE BEEN HONORED BY MR. SPOCK'S REQUEST THAT WE STAND WITH HIM AT HIS NUPTIAL CEREMONY.

Kirk, Spock and McCoy beam to the planet's surface...

...materializing a moment later in the dry, thin, 140 degree air of a normal Vulcan day.

There is a stark beauty about Spock's home planet, not lost upon Kirk and McCoy as they follow their shipmate across the alien landscape studded with weathered rock formations and glittering mica.

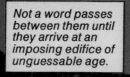

Not a word passes between them until they arrive at an imposing edifice of unguessable age.

This is the land of my family. It has been held by us for more than two thousand Earth years. This is our place of Koon-ut-kal-if-fee.

The structure before them is fascinating, comprised of contrasts. The pillored arena suggests the Stonehenge of ancient Earth, yet the mood, the atmosphere, is unique and unforgettable.

Koon-ut what?

He described it to me as meaning "marriage or challenge." In the distant past, Vulcans actually killed to win their mates.

Spock moves to the center of the enclosure and strikes the gong hanging above a glowing brazier of burnished stone, filling the air with a deep resonance.

GONNNGG!!

I never realized Vulcan was so lovely. But I do wish the atmosphere wasn't so thin, and that there was a cooler breeze.

Yeah, now I understand what they mean when they say, "Hot as Vulcan."

Less than a marriage, but more than a betrothal. Each touches the other in order to feel the other's thoughts. In this way our minds were locked together. And, at the proper time, we would both be drawn to Koon-ut-kal-if-fee

A formal procession enters the arena, with measured step and an air of ancient ritual.

Bones, do you see who that is?

She looks a little familiar.

Borne in a sedan chair at the head of the procession, a female Vulcan of dignified demeanor seems to exude authority from every pore.

It's T'Pau. The only person who ever turned down a seat on the Federation Council.

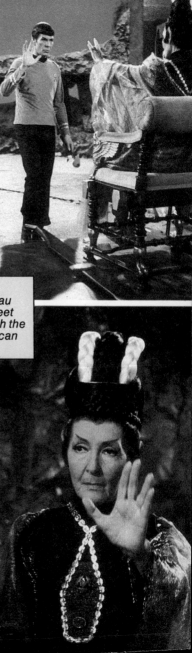

The two Vulcan women share a similar dignity; but while the sheer power of T'Pau's presence makes it difficult to meet her gaze, T'Pring's lithe grace invites scrutiny, and admiration.

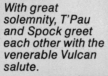

With great solemnity, T'Pau and Spock greet each other with the venerable Vulcan salute.

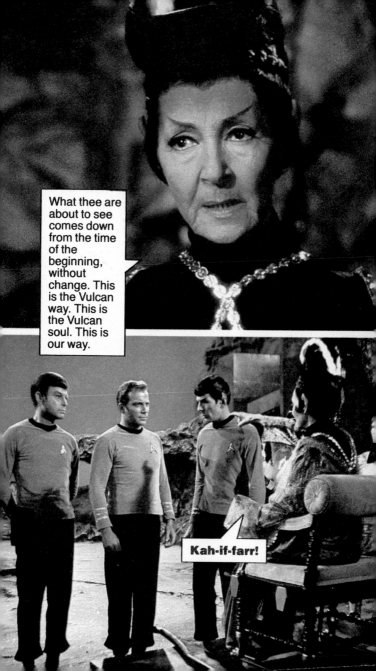

Kal-if-fee!

Thus, T'Pring exercises an ancient privilege.

And again the bells, their symbolism now apparent to both Kirk and McCoy.

Tling!

Kling Kling

Tling!

ng!

Kling!

Kling!

Ding!

Kling!

Kling Kling!

Tling!

Ding!

Stunned, for reasons not clear to his shipmates, Spock turns as if in a trance...

...and drops the mallet to the ground.

Spock withdraws deep into himself, concentrating his thoughts, his energies, his very being.

Do not attempt to speak with him. He is deep in the plak tow, the blood fever. He will not speak to you again until he has passed through what is to come.

Seeming oblivious to the proceedings, Spock's unswerving concentration is manifest in every line of his body.

Impassive,
T'Pring's serene
gaze reveals
nothing of her
feelings...

...but there are those whose thoughts can be read in their eyes.

Steeped in tradition, the ages-old preparations for ritual combat continue...

...as meaningful to Vulcans, as they are incomprehensible to outworlders.

The combatants are each presented with the "lirpa," a polished staff with a weighted cudgel at one end, surmounted by a razor-sharp crescent blade at the other.

Immersed in the plak tow, the blood fever, Spock is ready.

Nasty! Somebody could really get hurt with these.

I can forgive such a display only once. Challenge was given and lawfully accepted. It has begun. Let no one interfere.

It has indeed begun, in earnest!

As unfamiliar as he is with the weapon, Kirk's even greater handicap is the shock and horror of engaging in mortal combat with a friend.

Totally committed, Spock is unhampered by such considerations.

No match for Spock's Vulcan speed and power, Kirk's only chance is to go for a quick finish.

Spock reels from a blow...and Kirk leaps to press home the advantage.

Weakened by the hot, thin air, Kirk is unprepared for Spock's manic strength.

Kirk goes down hard, the wind knocked out of him, stunned, unable to rise.

Driven by the pon farr madness, Spock moves with amazing speed to deliver the death blow.

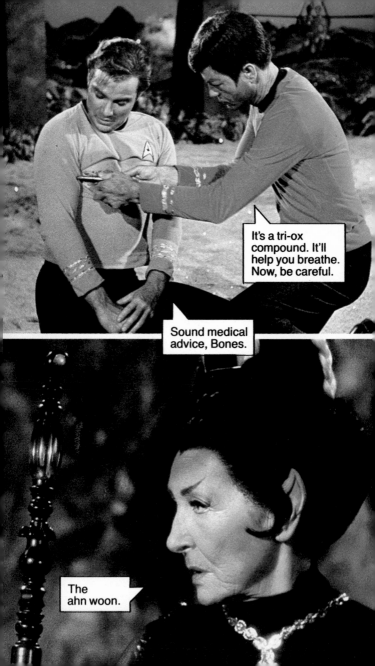

Kling

Ding!
Ding!
Ding!

Tling
Tling

Kling

Tling!
Kling!!

Kling
Klinga!

Heralding the second phase of ritual combat, the bells ring out again.

Kirk had heard of the ahn woon, the oldest of Vulcan weapons, but had never seen or touched one.

The ahn woon evoked memories for Spock, of his childhood on Vulcan. He was expert in its use as bola, sling and garrote.

Abruptly, the battle is joined as Spock, in one fluid movement, draws back and casts.

Spock's move, impossible to follow with the eye, is as fast as the strike of a Saurian sea snake...catching Kirk off guard, and tumbling him to the ground.

The raging fever in his blood seems to improve, rather than impair, Spock's fighting skill.

Using his weapon as a garrote, Spock tightens it about Kirk's throat, forcing him back into the glowing coals.

Kirk's trusted First Officer has become a killing machine.
Kirk can't stand much more. He's half gone now.

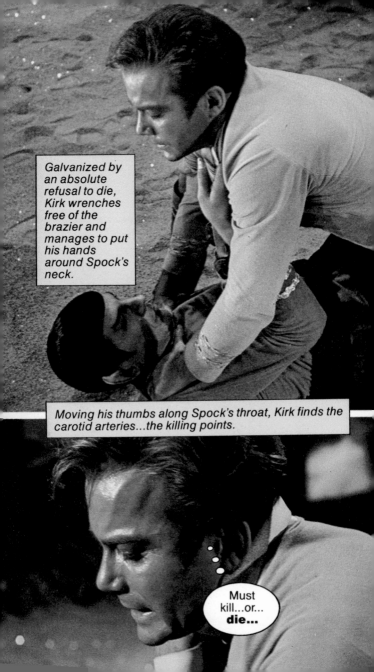

A sudden rasping gasp comes from Kirk's throat, forcing its way past the ahn woon around his neck...His grip loosens as his eyes roll up...and close.

Spock stands, retaining his grip on the ahn woon.

Kroykah!!

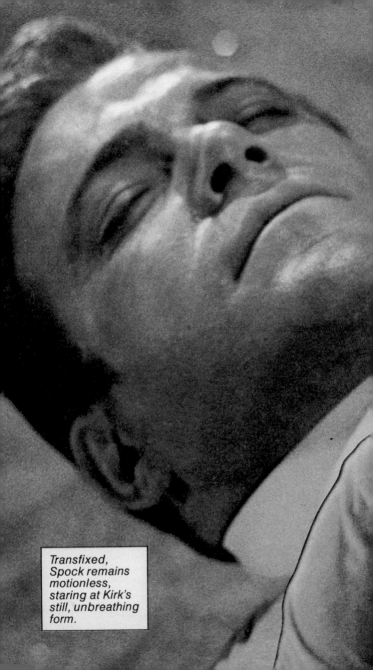

Transfixed, Spock remains motionless, staring at Kirk's still, unbreathing form.

Doctor McCoy rushes to Kirk and pushes Spock aside.

Get your hands off him, Spock!

It's finished. **He's dead!**

With Spock beamed safely aboard, the Enterprise *moves* out of orbit.

Spock locates Dr. McCoy in Sickbay.

Doctor, I shall be resigning my commission immediately. I would appreciate your making final arrangements—

Well, it's a little late, but I'm glad they're seeing it our way. Lt. Uhura, tell Mr. Chekov to lay in a course for Altair VI and leave orbit when ready. Kirk out.

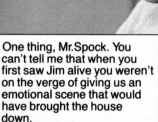

One thing, Mr. Spock. You can't tell me that when you first saw Jim alive you weren't on the verge of giving us an emotional scene that would have brought the house down.

Merely my quite logical relief that Star Fleet had not lost a highly proficient Captain.

I understand, Mr. Spock.

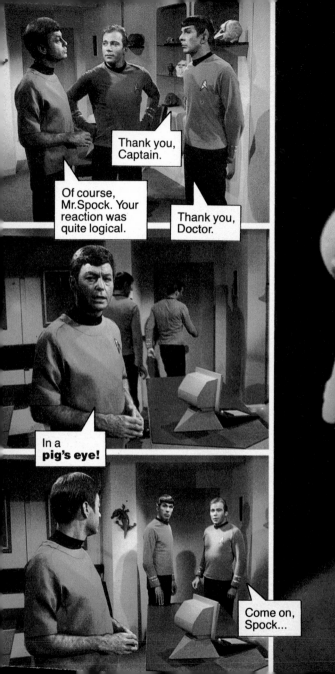

GLOSSARY

Bridge—The top deck of the Starship from which the Captain, his chief officers, and the navigator control the ship.

Captain's Log—Record keeping method used by the captain of all important activities affecting the Starship.

Sickbay—A compartment in the Starship located on the seventh deck and used as a dispensary and hospital.

Star Fleet Command—General headquarters where the command hierarchy is housed.

Transporter—Used to move crew and/or cargo from the Starship to planets and back by changing the object's original molecular structure into energy which can be beamed to a predetermined point where the original molecular formation can then be reconstructed.

Turbo-lift—Elevator-type compartments connecting all decks of the Starship. Capable of moving horizontally and vertically and operated either manually or by voice.

United Federation of Planets—Democratic alliance of planets comprised of several solar systems including Sol. All decisions affecting member planets are made through delegates to the Federation Council.

U.S.S. Enterprise—One of 13 Starships operated by the United Federation of Planets. This 190,000 metric ton craft, currently involved in a five year explorative mission, is crewed by approximately 430 people.

Viewscreens—Electronic devices positioned throughout the Starship that keep crew members in visual contact with each other. The main viewscreen is located on the ship's bridge and is capable of displaying in various magnifications all matter surrounding the ship's exterior.

Vulcan Mind Touch—A form of non-verbal communication passed from one mind to another perfected by Vulcans.

Vulcans—Race inhabiting the planet Vulcan. Recognizable by their pointed ears, upswept eyebrows and sallow complexion. A beautiful race known for their highly developed intelligence, strong sense of honor and their lack of emotionalism. Their lives are conducted through the use of logic and reason.

Warp Drive—Method of propulsion exceeding the speed of light.

STAR TREK QUIZ #8

In each question below, circle the one answer that best completes the sentence.

1. Kirk first becomes aware that something is wrong with Spock when:

a. Spock yells at Nurse Chapel

b. Spock refuses to answer Kirk's question

c. Spock asks for a leave of absence

d. Dr. McCoy reports a change in Spock's behavior

2. When Kirk asks Spock why he has changed the Starship's course, Spock tells him:

a. to leave him alone

b. he doesn't remember

c. he can't answer him

d. he had to

3. For a Vulcan, the pon farr is a time of:

a. madness

b. mating

c. challenge

d. killing

4. Kirk disobeys Admiral Komack's orders to head for Altair because:

a. the Starship isn't needed there

b. he knows he can get to Vulcan and then to Altair

c. Spock is his friend

d. Spock asks him to

5. T'Pau is:

a. Spock's wife

b. Spock's fiancé

c. The only woman to turn down a seat in the Federation Council

d. a member of Spock's family

6. One word that does not describe Vulcan air is:

a. dry

b. thin

c. hot

d. unbreathable

7. Kroykah means:

a. stop

b. blood fever

c. begin

d. challenge

8. Kirk agrees to fight Spock because:

a. he wants to prove something to T'Pau

b. he wants to prove something to T'Pring

c. he knows he can beat him

d. he knows Spock won't kill him

9. The first weapon used in the challenge is the:

a. plak tow

b. lirpa

c. ahn woon

d. cudgel

10. McCoy injects Kirk with:

a. a tri-ox compound

b. a neural paralyzer

c. quadro-triticale

d. cordrazene

Turn the page for the answers.

ANSWERS to Quiz on preceding pages:
1. **c.** 2. **b** 3. **b.** 4. **c.** 5. **c.** 6. **d.** 7. **a.** 8. **d.** 9. **b.** 10. **b.**